RIVER CHURCH

Selected Poems 1990 - 2025

KENT FIELDING

Radial Books

Also by Kent Fielding
Chief Iffucan
The Revolution is About to Begin, with Ron Whitehead
Before the Grave, Editor
Once Removed, Editor
Critical Interpretations on Fear and Loathing in Las Vegas, Editor

Cover Artwork: *Long Bay* by Adalia Deach, 2024.

Published by Radial Books
radialbooks.org

River Church / Kent Fielding, 1st ed.

ISBN: 979-8-9907540-1-0

ACKNOWLEDGEMENTS

The author would like to thank the following publications where some of these poems first appeared.

"Confessions of Snow" in *Keeping the Flame Alive #8*

"Raining Fish" in *Yearling: A Poetry Journal for Working Writers*

"Lessons in Fairbanks" in *The Rye Whiskey Review*

"Hangover" in *The Rye Whiskey Review*

"Stealing Time" in *Bronze Bird Review*

"Violent Extinction of Stars" in *Keeping the Flame Alive #4*

"Kansas City Airport" in *The Rye Whiskey Review*

"Moon" in *Fallen Vol. 1*

"The Grey of the World" and "Kentucky" in *Night Owl Narrative Vol. 4*

"Asleep in Ust-Ilismk, Siberia," "Nightmare," and "Bessie" in *Night Owl Narrative Vol. 3*

"The Lover" in *Skagway News* published in a different form as "The Brief Affair" in *Lungfull Issue 14*

"Museums" as a Cheek Press Broadside

"White Trash" and "Caught in Winter" in *Tidal Echoes*

"Callia" in *Prism Magazine*

"The Goat Woman's Dream: Joan of Arc" in *The World Healing Book.*

"An Overheard Conversation Outside Denny's in Anchorage 5 a.m." in *Frisk Magazine*

"Her Breasts Were Loud" and "I Have Never Married" in *Pavement Saw #6*

"Drinking Alone" in *Prairie Schooner*, Alaska Literature Issue

"Fantasia" in *Time All Over: An Anthology of Kentucky Poets and Visual Artists.*

"Corning" and "Named" in *The Jefferson Review*

"Security Report #211" in *Boog Magazine*

To Este, Callia, and Amara

CONTENTS

I: STEALING TIME

COFFEE WITH ADELE

She slips coffee as a bluejay lands
in a nearby tree. My aunt is 102.

She does not recognize me, does
not remember all the times I turned her

mattress, washed her car, brought her the chocolate
brownies she's not allowed to eat, but

she tells me about her family's farm,
the horses, the barn, the cows on the hill, all the chores,

how she desperately wanted to escape the country,
escape the tobacco hanging in the barn, and the smell of
        manure,

she explains what it was like to live through World
            War II—
the cousin who lost his leg at Omaha Beach, how he no
        longer

laughed or smiled but was quiet, hollow. How she read
            newspapers—
searching for names of friends killed, missing, searching

for her cousin's missing leg. How she moved to the
            city,
waited tables at a diner—how she met her husband,
        Ted.

"After Macy's Thanksgiving Parade, at a bar he bought
me a drink. He was Irish, a fireman, loved his whiskey

and he could laugh. He could tell a story and always
smelled like peppermint." She smiles at the thoughts of
        him.

3

I'm told that each memory is its own world, formed,
and reformed every time we create it—

as if experienced for the first time,
as if imagined for the first time, again,

and again, and again. "Who are you?"
she asks, "I forgot your name."

And I begin to think about my own aging—
disappearing into dates and images of the past,

unable to recognize family in the present. What does
it mean to be alive but lost

To remember yesterdays but not what happened an hour
          ago?
Will I vividly remember the 1980s, the songs of Michael
          Jackson,

Kurt Cobain's suicide, the first girl who kissed me,
and who broke my heart, but forget

my granddaughter's face?
                              Will my
                    granddaughter sit
next to me
              a stranger drinking coffee?

Will I listen
              to birdsongs
                              watch

the clouds

                    alone?

ASLEEP IN UST-ILIMSK, SIBERIA

My girlfriend does not believe in kissing. She wants me
to commit suicide during the act of love. She believes
       death and sex should be connected.

Death is but the echo of sex, she says *or is it the other way:*
sex is but the dream of death, and death eventually wakes up.

The resting heart beats: silence after thunder.
Silence after thunder is the mouth of the river.

As an old man, my bowl is filled with the bulbs
of lightning bugs, thousands upon thousands. I spoon
       the beads into my mouth,

chew the light, swallow the light, digest the light
until all the light of the world is inside me

and everything goes dark.

NAMED: KENT

Think of cigarettes
"Your father named you
after his favorite brand."
My uncle chuckles,
sipping Wild Turkey.
My father, a chronic smoker, smoked
nine packs during my mother's labor.
The story: he stood staring
at a pack—Kent 100s—
when the nurse brought
the news: "A boy."
Think of cigarettes.
Think of my father, the white
lobby, his pacing, stick
after stick in his mouth,
smoke curling from his lips
like rough ocean waves on a foggy
morning. Think of cigarettes.
Think of me. Named after his
favorite brand: I became the smoke
that made my father cough,
the smoke that blackened lungs,
the smoke that filled
the long work hours
at a school he hated—inhale, inhale—
to buy bread, to buy shoes
we were poor, we needed
so many things: pencils, pants,
doctor visits, dental work
electricity, heat, milk. Love.
I am the smoke-filled days
the orange flare as he inhaled.
My growth and deeds became stubs
that looked like tombstones
in the ashtray. I got in fights at school
with kids older, gave one ten

stitches, threw rocks at cars
nicking and denting two or three.
I stole candy from stores,
peed on my 2nd grade teacher's
Datsun, hid in the woods
to avoid the principal and a whipping.
Still my father came, reliable, stern
again and again, he came
to get me from the office
cigarette stuck in the corner
of his mouth, gray smoke
drifting into his graying hair.
Again and again, he inhaled,
asked, "What were you thinking?"
I think of the cigarettes
in his hands—chalk sticks
to mist one's name. Our lives
are the inhale of burning particles.
Our lives are the release of gray truths.
When I die let it be with smoke & fire.
Let the consumption be brief.
Think of cigarettes.
Think of my father
working into the night
grading papers, shaking his head,
missing sleep, so that I could eat,
so that he could protect me,
so that I could grow and learn.
Think of the smoke in his lungs.
The smoke that ate his life.

STEALING TIME

You must make the time to write—
steal it from somewhere
from employers who believe they
own the minutes of your life,
silently say, "These are my moments"
and write. Write lines during day as you
answer the phone, teach students,
wait on tables, lay concrete—
record it, write it. You own your seconds
no matter how much someone pays
you. Write during sleep—dream
poetry and get up in the night
to protect the words. Write during
chores, turn that grocery list
into a poem: tomatoes, carrots
and the yolk of the moon
scrambled into daylight.
Make your life yours again.
Stay away from people who want
to own you, or who need your attention,
who need your gossip, your time,
your energy, who want to sell
you something. Write a "I'm done with you"
poem. Start it: "Dear so and so,
Look for worms in the earth. Smell the
earth. I am of the earth. I am the earth."

NIGHTMARE

Once I awoke on a train—
a man sat drinking Russian Vodka
his face was a coffin: his mother's coffin
and his mouth was the lid of that coffin.
It opened and shut as he drank,
opened and shut as if a line of people
examined the body, said their goodbyes,
closed the casket and allowed the next to open it.
But the mother died in a fire and there was nothing
but ash, and there was ash in the man's mouth
it overflowed and fell onto his shirt.
He tried to wash the ash down with vodka.
The more he drank, the more ash appeared,
therefore, he drank more and more. The ash multiplied
as if the mother said, "No more. I come back now.
Stop this. No more. You shouldn't have swallowed me.
I come back." The ash became like a stream.
It ran off his chin and into his lap.
One might think the ash was vomit.
The man kept repeating, "I give up my soul.
I give up my soul, mama. It burnt with you."
He choked on the ash and swallowed the vodka.
The train entered a very long tunnel.

THE LOVER

When I met the girl in the tobacco field
the rain descended with angry insults.
It did not like our affair and appeared jealous.
The rain did not believe I was her husband.
It wanted her for itself. The water beads
turned into worms, centipedes, maggots.
They crawled in my hair, on my skin, and bit.
Thunder rolled like an older and harsher voice,
an oak cracked in two. We ran laughing to a barn
where we undressed for the rain.

*

Later, my heart became a trout
pulled from a deep lake. I felt
a knife filleted it for the frying pan.
There was the smell of garlic and onion.
The olive oil sizzled, a series of kisses
from a happy mouth, the flesh smiled
as it fried. And there were leftovers
for a week. The girl had never eaten
such a fish. She walked home full and the
rain hugged her and called her "daughter."

CALLIA

Conceived during an electrical storm,
cracks of energy ripped the dark canvas,
and you willed your way into your mother's laughter,
floated in her ocean dream as your father taught,
his voice some faraway murmur:
summer sounds of something above the waves.
They told him you had come to break his heart.
They told him you were his comet.
All afternoon in the tropical light
on those islands in the remote Pacific,
He worked his English magic, turned words
into water, turned water into wind,
and wind into the breath of trees:
the leafy palms that floated in his dreams.
As nights he turned in his sweated sheets,
as he worried about you, about what you
meant in his lost boyhood, his lost last calls
when the alcohol became too much and he
settled into a marriage with a woman
as fierce as a flooded river, who followed
his endless wanderings, with endless love
with endless forgiveness for all the wrong
paths, the trails that took him into the brambles
that disappeared into snow, disappeared into ocean
foam, at the foot of icy mountains. Then you came
and he could no longer wander without
your weight in his arms, your squeal,
your laughter, your sleeping, your coos
to go that next block, to see the grass, the trees,
the dog again, to hear the crickets.
His happiness became the white moon of your voice.

KANSAS CITY AIRPORT

She sits at the bar
drinking a beer, empty shot
glass near her right hand.
It's 5 a.m. and she is alone.
Her feet are on a nearby
stool. Her lips are forming
the words, "Who the fuck cares."
What are these moments—
the 5 a.m. need for a drink
in a town she is escaping.
The desire to flee from thought
from emotion, from the man
she has just left with the handwritten
note: *Mark, you are not good*
in bed, you are not good with your hands
on my body or anywhere else.
You are not good at commitment.
Love is about doing things for another
when it is needed.
Even if you don't
want to do those things.
You don't know how
to change the oil in a car,
vacuum or mop a floor,
cook an egg. Did we really
just fall in love conjugating
verbs in Latin class?
It's 2 a.m. and I'm getting
on a flight in four hours,
and I'm better at saying goodbye
than you. Remember our old saying,
It is better to drink off a good
sleep than to meet the day. Remember
that when you wake, there's whiskey
in the cabinet. I left shot glasses
on the table. Take care of yourself.

You don't do that well either.
Here is to two years. Love,
Rebecca. The bartender is
still opening for the morning
breakfast rush and the potential
Bloody-Mary. The girl, Rebecca,
raises her hand and motions
for another round.

BESSIE

My cousin of the halibut
was an excellent lover.
We lay in bed under sheets
and spoke each other's names,
touched each other's bruises,
rubbed the good and the bad
of our lives.
When we kissed our tongues—
candles for caverns—flared,
our arms—rails
for the storms—creaked.
Our thoughts became seas
upon which we floated.
Neither of us remembered
when we had lived.

MOON

We are at the bottom of a deep well.
We look up at the opening:

the rich white light
like the ghost of a perfect day

that we can't forgive,
but through that hole it's day

all the time. The light as loud
as a wall of skulls.

We wonder how to get out.
We wonder how long we've

been down here trapped in the dark.
Why have we been forgotten?

Where are the rescue squads?
At times we climb towards the light,

and it becomes the mouth of our mother:
come closer, she says.

You can do it, she says.
But the mouth has teeth,

and she wishes to swallow us.
At times it is a distant fire

that reminds us
how cold we have become—

we wish to thaw.
At times we hear voices

beyond its gap, there are kids playing.
We call out—we're here, hello!

But no one answers.
Why are we so alone?

CONFESSIONS OF SNOW

I.

Snowmen talk
in whispers, romantic and dark,
discuss their former lives
as water, as cloud vapor,
their miraculous birth
as frozen crystals
waltzing through winter air. Air
cold enough to freeze lungs.
Their bodies molded by children
on a break from school—
laughter bringing them awake
out of the dark—innocent,
they talk of shadows,
they talk of moonlight
on the whiteness of wintry earth.

Their mouths are made of buckwheat
coal found by railroads.
Their words full of industry and carbon,
business and profit.
They repeat what they hear.
"Business is good for the world."
Buttons for eyes and scarves
wrapped around their necks
by careful mothers; a pipe
from a father's study—to smoke
tobacco leftover in the bowl. They learn
early, fire is important. Fire is bright.

II.

After a few days
witnessing snowball fights,

they become family:
the adopted uncle,
always nearby,
always ready,
to tell the wild joke: how do
snowmen mate? With ice-
testicles. Only the frozen stars laugh
at their humor. The snowmen begin to demand:
"Call us snow people." They
say, "Where are the snowwomen?"
"We want snowwomen,
and puppies. We want
equal rights and jobs.
We want families.
We have rights."

III.

As they age, snowmen become
lecherous. Empty beer
cans surround them in
the morning and
the whiff of marijuana smoke
drifts through their hats.
They demand to be kissed.
They demand snowman-caves
to hang out with other snowmen,
to watch snow sports and drink
cheap Canadian whiskey.
Their laughter is Abraham Lincoln
splitting logs after midnight
in the glow of a lantern and
after the secession of Southern States.

Outside of bedrooms
they watch women
and men undress.
Their stick hands long
to touch flesh. They begin

to comprehend desire,
and with desire
begins all deaths.

IV.

Yet, at night
under a bone-white moon—full,
if you listen closely,
they'll teach you
about absence.
They'll teach you
about stillness.
They'll teach you
how to be alone.

TEACHERS

—In memory of Raymond Stein, a friend

In the South Pacific
Coral reefs, turquoise from sky,
grow upon the rims of extinct
volcanoes, upon dead coral.
These gardens provide habitat
for schools of yellow fin dancing
in orchestrated swirls of light
ballet and harmony like ideals
balanced in some cherub's song
here eels play hide and seek
in holes and butterfly fish flutter
like men dreaming of worlds
beyond their breath
where jellyfish float like ghosts
of miniature fortresses
where men battled for
religion or an afterlife.
Sea fans spread and seaweed
reach arms toward the sun
while polyps and crabs
scuttle the silent floor of sand.
Here in this Eden, God's wisdom
comes forth in colors: blue, purple, green.
For when coral dies, new coral grows,
coral upon coral for years
until out of the sea white land emerges
an island pushed out of the womb
innocent and new, a baby waking
in the morning of the first day.
The wind and waves carry seeds
and slowly life takes new shapes:
coarse grass spreads like a rash

followed by hibiscus and then trees:
breadfruit and palm. Turtles lay
eggs on the beach. Birds—heron,
sandpiper, tern—migrate and build.
Snails, beetles, lizards, toads, rats appear.
until the wild issues forth its own voice...

In a similar way, I think of a teacher
as a coral reef, as a garden underwater
he keeps the important spirit alive
beneath the surface, he nourishes
he provides, he protects
his classroom is the calm of water
where ideas like plankton take in light
and grow into larger fish, into larger beings.
The teacher directs, the teacher cultivates
and finally, the teacher pushes forth
islands into the sun to become their
own gardens, their own patches of life.

WHITE TRASH

Two sisters, twelve and ten
tears streaming down their cheeks
stand in their front yard
before them, the neighborhood boys
pick though their family's trash—a washing machine,
        clothes,
boxes filled with every toy they own:
Barbie dolls, Cabbage Patch Kids, Slinkys,
Lego blocks, plastic army soldiers, G.I. Joes,
cast-metal fire trucks.

                              Last night their father
brain, whiskey-fired, a bonfire burning all winter's
        wood,
sat at a game, drew a full-house aces high
felt like a teenager on a Saturday-night car ride, free,
        speeding the back roads
wild and still time to change the world, still time to be
        that American hero
dizzy with action, confidence, and youthful looks
wished he had a farm to bet or at least a herd of cattle
felt the money multiplying in his pockets like a barn of
        cats all meowing
wanted to shout to his daddy, "I ain't no loser, you were
        wrong Daddy-O
this cat's escaping the gutter, going out on the town.
Gonna buy that new Cadillac"
threw a thousand down, yelled, "CALL" and danced a
        drink down his throat
watched five spades: Ten, Jack, Queen, King, Ace
throw dirt on him bury him in the churchyard with a
        small square stone:
Here rests Harold, his vision dull and useless
took it as a sign, a meteor burning in his veins:
God is watching. My family owns too much.
Went home where his tongue became sandpaper

roughed up the smooth, quiet air:
"Spoiled brats," he woke the girls from dreams of snow
                forts,
"You have. You have and don't appreciate."
Hurled a whiskey pint through window
jagged glass hung, shards fell
from the girls' eyes as they huddled in bed.
"Harold," Mother screamed, "Who's gonna clean
                that?"
At 3 a.m., the white curtain night, full bone of moon
and their father's voice a fist
they picked up every possession they owned
dumped them in boxes of cardboard, dragged to street,
watched, as father snored whiskey from body,
watched the morning red creep into the world, a flame,
an announcement
Nothing's ever going to change, no one's every going to come
No white knight, no good Christian, no cigarette-smoking
                cowboy
Not even a longhaired stoned revolutionary nodding
                "PEACE"
Only the ghosts of cemeteries will be our friends
Watched as the young, unwashed neighborhood boys,
gathered at their door to take the G.I. Joes, the Slinkys,
take the Barbie dolls for BB gun practice,
take the Cabbage Patch dolls to burn, take all they own
asking, "You're throwing these out?"
The girls nod, "We don't need them anymore."

MUSEUMS

I often visit thrift stores
to purchase second hand trophies,
any odd trophy:
the winner of a free throw contest,
bowling trophies, soccer trophies,
a trophy from a county fair: *1992 Owen County
Best Chili.* Dancing trophies or even medals of races,
like marathons, run, regardless of time
or placing. Anything with someone
else's name. I want to visit other lives,
live other successes—those brief
moments of triumph against lifetimes
of ordinary moments. But who defines
what is ordinary? Is anything ordinary?
Likewise, I look for items
that suggest failures—lost marriages,
lost jobs, misplaced childhoods,
and the struggles of day-to-day existence.
Sometimes I find picture frames
with the photos still left:
a man and woman with two blonde children,
a boy and girl, before a small brick home
in a day filled with sun.
The woman has a smile on her face. The man
has confidence in his eyes. He is clean shaven.
In the moment, he looks like a winner.
But it is only a moment.
Or I'll look for books with dedications signed
inside the front cover:
Remember that night in Pittsburg,
how we woke the entire hotel with our love,
our laughter. I remembered
you liked Thomas Wolfe –Beth.
And I can see the hotel,
a night after the theater, the wine,
the moaning like an air raid. Someone pounding

on the wall to shut them up.
I can even hear the phone, see the hand
that knocks the receiver to the floor.
And I can imagine the two
going separate ways—the distance,
the lack of communication over the years,
the disconnection that brings the book to this shelf.
And what about jewelry—necklaces
like jade or pearls bought in some foreign country
on some grand trip, or engraved rings:
To My Beloved on our 25th. Was there a 30th?
How long were they married? Are they still alive?
Who dropped off the donation?
Or coffee mugs—"World's Best Grandma"
or even those unique pieces of clothing:
the brown suit coat with patches over the elbows
with notes for a speech still in the inside pocket.
*Today I would like to thank all those who gathered in this
        hall…*
The sunlight of the day is brief.

II: FROM K's MEMOIRS

I HAVE NEVER MARRIED

D. lived in a faraway country. She often wrote me love
letters full of storms: windstorms on lakes full of large
waves that sunk fishing boats; tornadoes in the plains
that sucked up cattle; thunderstorms that flooded small
towns and drowned family dogs; lightning storms in
New Mexico with fingers of light searching for moist
trees; blizzards in Alaska that buried couples on
honeymoons. A very passionate lover, she drowned
in the river one Fall in a freak canoe accident. The
police blamed the clouds, the voices in the clouds. Said
it was "cloud activity" and expected graffiti to form on
the streets. She comes back now in my dreams of
gardens. She stands among the rows of peas and
cauliflower and whispers, "My dear husband, my dear
lost husband." Often in these dreams we chat about the
weather. How it is always sunny where she now lives,
and the children do not worry about dark or stories of
wolves. I have never married. I once dated an editor—
she had a language of pine needles and her breath
always smelled sharp green. We took long dinners over
bottles of red wine in the woods of white oak under the
chirps of squirrels and we talked about Hayden Carruth
and Gregory Corso. Poets of dark tunnels of roots
grown underwater. We talked until the crickets put
away their legs and the roosters announced dusk. I
believed I lusted after her. Wanted her to touch the tree
of knowledge that rested in the field of weeds. Its gate
rusted and left unlocked, the Angel guard on vacation. It
was thus my surprise when my lust was returned in a
form letter:

> Sorry we cannot use your lust at this time.
> Please think of us again in the future.

It was not even signed. D. tells me she is the only one for me and since she is dead, I am dead. I have never married.

WITH KIM, CLARKSVILLE, TN

We sat in a hillbilly bar
filled with bottled beer, pool
tables, men in steel-
toed boots, who smoked
Marlboros through facial
hair and raised every
other word into a curse.
Kim, having skin the color
of Langston's rivers
hated the place with good
reason: this was a town
where every now and then
they still stomped an inter-
racial couple, just for practice.
But, her boyfriend, an Army
boy, hung out at every other
bar, and, according to her
carried a blade with a jealous
grip.

      We watched these blue
collared boys get ripped,
while we talked Miles
Davis and "The Birth of
the Cool." How one art
style emerges into another,
how breaks, no matter how
subtle are necessary for growth.
Cue balls smacked apart
the organized solids and stripes,
as table after table was stripped
clean and then reorganized.
My own girlfriend was back
in Louisville, probably at a bar
discussing literature
getting so drunk she'd stumble

home, slip under the covers
naked, waiting to be touched.
We had shared our hatreds of each
other—the everything she wanted,
the nothing I seemed to care about.

Kim and I dissected each other's
hands. She had a love line with
many deep fissures, an army of
breaks and bad men. I had
a path that seemed to travel
uninterrupted—on and on
like a highway in Iowa.
We drove back to the Hotel 6
where I lit as many candles
as I could find at 2 a.m.
in a Dairy Mart along a dark
Cumberland River. Then
without guilt, I pulled off
her Bulls jersey, Jordan
on the back, and unbuckled
her jeans, slipped them down to reveal
thighs. We did not question the return
to other mates, nor what this act
meant about those ties. We
pounded each other into moans
until the sun broke day, then slept
skin against skin, palm against
palm. The next day I returned north,
drove back through Western Kentucky's
stripped-mined earth, the broken
land barren, painful in the light.
Drove back through the tobacco of
Central Kentucky, back to the four
a.m. drunks and two more years
of fights.

IN HER BREASTS, A STEREO

A stereo existed in her breasts.
He could put his ear to each
as if each were a speaker
and catch Sarah Vaughan or Robert
Johnson or the baseball game.
He loved how she could channel
the world through her body—
except on some nights, some nights
when she shed her clothes
the frequency became too loud
too clear, too much.
He'd hear the news, "212 dead in a plane
Crash," or punk music
"I'm gonna cut your throat"
things he did not want—
threatening things and he would
try to kiss the speakers into moans.
She'd whisper *I'm lonely, I need more.*
Once he came home to an angry L.A.
protest coming out of her.
A street mob outside a Levi's factory
filled the room—he began to see
each face as it marched his wooden floor
he saw the brown skin emerge
from the shadows, rage flared in the eyes
and the distorted mouths broke in shouts:

> "Our families are starving,
> And they're cutting our pay
> More respect for common people"

Fifteen or twenty bodies
marched around, carried signs
"Boycott Levi" "Latino Workers make your jeans"
"More than minimum wage."
Police soon broke down his door to arrest

the protesters, handcuff, and billy club them
he watched as they hauled away bodies
night bruised with screams.
                    I'm lonely.
The woman he loved sat naked on the couch
he approached her, rubbed her nipples
softly, twisted them softly, turned them
to turn down the noise, turn down
so the neighbors might not hear.

GIRL ON A TRAMPOLINE

Growing up, my neighbor owned a trampoline, and had
a daughter. I don't believe the daughter was rebellious; I
remember her as a straight-A student, honor roll,
National Honors Society, played field hockey or some
other outdoor sport. One year, after she'd been away at
college, there were rumors of break-up with a
boyfriend—she found him with her best friend and
another girl, a threesome or something, and she had
started to do acid. Rumors that maybe I heard or made
sense of later. I remember seeing her that summer
jumping on a trampoline. I had just turned ten. I was
outside, eating green Jell-O, back against the warm brick
wall of my house, the sun bright, the trees leafy green.
She wore a black dress, or skirt, that was inches above
her knees, but as she jumped and came down from those
heights of her bounces, the dress rose above her thighs
and parachuted out. As I started to watch her jump, I
suddenly realized that she wasn't wearing under
garments—the dark triangle of pubic hair and her
tanned thighs appeared. Her pubic hair, that region,
seemed to have its own identity. I froze realizing I was
witnessing some taboo, the neighbor's daughter, the
innocent girl next door, playing Marilyn Monroe; her
dress blown upwards, exposing what was hidden
underneath. Excited, confused, my heart accelerated,
blood pressure rose, and suddenly, I realized that she
was watching me; she was smiling—she was aware, had
been aware the entire time, that I was watching and that
she was corrupting me, and she enjoyed it. She really
enjoyed it. I could see her laugh.

Years later, when I kissed girlfriends, made out with
girlfriends, and began removing their clothes, I saw her
on that trampoline. She watched and smiled as I kissed
their skin, as I started to make love to their bodies. She
was there, always there, watching.

CAUGHT IN WINTER

I wanted to tell her about my neighbor,
The one who watched dog teams race through
paper birch, black spruce, near her cabin
when the snow became deep. The neighbor
who smoked in forty below, shook in a thin
jacket, then filled the woods with his release, "I'm
       alive!"
The neighbor who went cross-country skiing
was buried in an avalanche of a mountain's
awakening: Spring's first shiver.
How he told me the weekend before,
"Can't go up there. Too dangerous, too much snow.
A mountain can only hold so much." But still he went,
wanted to see the peace of it, the beauty of it,
the moon whose pulse reaches out to kiss,
illuminate snow, light captured within
the drift's glimmer. I remember how
the rescuers described the event:
the fury of being caught in that white wave
as it swept over him at a hundred miles an hour,
dragged him along. How his hand broke the snow's
surface where it left him. A blue-gloved fist
sticking up like a flag, a sign of defiance,
a last hope that someone would find him,
pull him out.
               And they did, four days too late.
His eyes frozen open, brown pupils faded to grey,
his mouth full of ice as lungs had sucked in snow
in final effort. In his disappearing breath,
did the depleted oxygen uncover suffocated thoughts?
A desire to tell a mother, *I'm sorry; sorry for leaving
so many times, with no contact.*

I wanted to tell her about his cabin in the woods.
How he built it, cut, and hauled the logs
up the small ridge, up on the edge of Ester Dome,

up where trees bend with snow's weight,
where moose wander freely in winter's dark.
He covered the gaps with pitch, cut windows
in the right direction—South—so the small room
would receive all of winter's brief light.
He had planned his own shifting there,
some map of future moments, some calculation
of the importance of choice and lifestyle.
I wanted to tell her how my friend Joanna
bought the land from his mother, his mother
who refused the trip, refused to understand
how he lived, maybe why he died.
How Joanna let the land he cleared heal,
grow over his invasion, cover up his intrusion,
and the cabin slowly decayed with weather
and time like a body left out in the open air.

I wanted to tell her that the beauty of a winter
mountain is the knowledge of its brevity, its power.
It is a symbol of life against which we all rebel
as we get sucked under in its white roar.

CORNING

Sundays were made for rain:
The black clouds, faces of the dead,
the ignored cemetery at the edge of town:
Corning, to live here your skin most welcome
cold, icy fingers massaging bones, bare
branches whipping with snow-filled
wind, creatures who lack mouths or tongues.
Here whiskey is whispered in the evening
at oak bars among the men,
who talk about fire, burning abandoned houses,
anything to induce heat, sweat is dangerous
but welcomed, like women, like kisses.
They say the steel mills have cancer,
people will soon move—
"It's those damn Chinese!"
Nods. People here are controlled by hunger.
The low growl of their stomachs
turning, turning, turning like the swirl of storms.
In the Spring rain falls and snow melts like wax.

FLORIDA FISHER

A bruise the shape of Europe
on the woman's bicep
as the coffee perks, as she flips
pancakes. The man, pulling on a ball cap
walks the path through cypress, sycamore—
trees whose roots cling to lakes
and rivers. The worn trail
brushy with overgrown blackberry brambles
with vines and Spanish moss,
green tinsel strangling trees.
The man has been careless
failed to trim his way to water
to the old rowboat on the swamp bank
the old rowboat which is his heart
the crinkling oars sliding through algae
the rhythm of his blood. He hears
the paper-bag voice of his wife, "Breakfast,"
lights a cigarette under mustached lip
sees a falcon fall with outstretched talons.
His own knuckles moan: black, bloody.

HANGOVER

As a young man I used to tell people
all good things involve sweat
and of course, I meant workouts
and spicy food, and sex
(skin upon skin, steam bath-like rooms,
damp hair, the taste of salt on the tongue,
wrestling, moaning, collision-rough sweat).
I suppose I even meant hangovers.
I used to find satisfaction in those after-mornings.
The survival of poison, the body's ability
to remove toxins, to purify itself
with its own water—holy perhaps,
as all survival is holy.

AFTER MY FRIEND'S DEATH

Two days, drinking continuously
I packed his office:

unplugged the computer,
disconnected wires of electricity,

turned off data, numbers, years
of financial statements,

boxed up journals of daily words,
journals of plans, journals of letters,

outlines, definitions of obscure words
he planned to use,

dreams he captured upon waking:
"And I found myself in a forest of light

with my wife and we danced to a violin…"
boxed up a diary—the last date 10/16/02—

two weeks before
boxed up his life to be stored, hidden,

saved as if someone would remember.

LESSONS IN FAIRBANKS

The double-wide
trailer with bright lamps
shining through the falling snow
served as a massage parlor.
Only two girls worked, and a
thick bearded man smoked a cigar,
the orange end blazed as he smiled.
A fair-skinned blonde took me
to a back room rubbed in hot oil and said,
"For a hundred you can do anything."
The woman must have been thirty-
five and wore heavy perfume
that smelled like baby powder.
She held my hands, kissed my cheeks,
stuck her tongue in my ear and whispered
warm words: you're handsome,
your legs are strong, what woman
wouldn't want you?
Someone somewhere
must have loved her and wondered.
She must have had a mother,
a father, and maybe a lover
who knew and understood.
Against me her skin perspired
as I grunted and thrust against her
To me she was a weapon
a chainsaw, gasoline, a bomb.
Something to drain all my aggression
to take out all my loneliness and pain
to get rid of the winter inside.
I'd been separated two months
My ex-girl, the one I planned
to marry, was in Spokane,
living with another man
the breakup had come in email
distance is too great, too lonely

the world then froze: blue-black
night, thirty below with white
birches and ice fog.
Darkness that did not vanish.

CONFESSION

In the lacquered box, I listened to the priest's voice
distant like gravediggers on a faraway hill.
What is your sin, my son? What do you wish to tell God?
The sounds of shovels lifting dirt and faces smeared with
       black grit.
Because I had nothing to confess, my life just blue sky,
I told the priest that I'd killed the old man downstairs,
knocked on his door with a butcher
knife, stabbed him ten times when he answered,
ripped open his chest because he never smiled.
Because he carried gray skin and dark moles, because he
       stared at people
with eyes like two closets full of hidden manuscripts.
Manuscripts of dead horses and maggots,
words which called forth rain and war against heaven.
After the old man's death, I slept with his dark-skinned
       daughter.
The one who once dropped letters out the window and
       lit herself on fire.
The one who met me on the stairs and held my hands to
       her face.
I am too much like my mother, she whispered, *too alive.*
We made love on the straw mattress, smeared each
       other with blood,
rubbed ourselves into crimson skies. Then, I walked to
       church.

I bang on the box walls, try to startle the priest
       I do not want God's forgiveness, Father,
I want him to call me out, to critique my life, my words,
my sentences, to say, "This image is good. It will last."

KFC INTERNATIONAL HEADQUARTERS: SECURITY REPORT NO. 211

At 0100 hours on Friday October 29th this security officer spotted a couple dressed drag, Marilyn Monroe and Lucille Ball wearing too much lipstick and eye shadow, out by the gazebo feeding Rainbow Bread to the ducks and remarking how a few "looked like chickens." I failed to inform them of the crossbreeding experiments. Our basement labs filled with thousands of eggs and incubators. The couple stood a moment laughing in white ballroom dresses, rolling the bread into balls. Our pond a smile. The White House on the hill a flexed bicep. The Technological Center a barracks. The moon appeared a halo above our grounds and two geese swam like dancers in the background as the wing-clipped ducks climbed banks yelling like a bunch of children. I told the couple they were on private property and read them the NO TRESPASSING HAIKU:

> Police with billy clubs
> swing wildly at heads, kick ribs.
> They get free chicken.

The women, oddly in tennis shoes, got quiet, admitted their ignorance, saying they were from Georgia, Bacon County—Hog Capital—and nodded penitence. One offered me the lilac from her wig. I recited rule 7 of the KFC Security Officer's Handbook: "Accept No Gifts While On Duty. Asterisk: especially from men posed as women." I thought of the original recipe bank vaulted on the second floor of the White House near a CEO's office and how ungodly important it was, and I quickly walked the women to their red Chevrolet Cavalier, noted the dented right fender, the broken right sideview mirror, and called the license plate number into Security Officer Rose. He recorded it for posterity. Marilyn said she liked a man in uniform and blew me a kiss. She lit a cigarette, rolled up the window, and the car darted off like a herd of unbroke horses breaking our 10-mph speed limit and running two stop signs before squealing onto Prospect Road. This officer suggests gassing them with cockroach poison if they ever return. I finished my tour with no other incidents. Stopped briefly to watch the two willows in the SE corner flap their limbs in wild prayer—hundreds of worshippers bowing near our gates. Our moon a halo. Our stock up 3 pts. In his sincere protection of Colonel Sanders Land in the Kingdom of KFC,

Security Officer Johnson Fiddle

FANTASIA

Behind Disney's World
a dead orange orchard
trees twisted and blackened—
bent monks shrieking too much light
after meditating for years in darkness—
twisted and blackened,
exposed roots knotted, gnarled:
by chemicals.
Desert without lizards,
nomads or music,
next to the road
only the employees use.

KWAJALEIN

The orange flame of sun
extinguishes itself in ocean,
a neon basketball in
a gym going dark,
the scoreboard's red lights reading
Home 49, Visitors 50.
Someone, somewhere, has lost
and goes home with head down,
goes home to eat cold soup alone
in the dark of a one room shack.
A couple on bicycles, Americans,
wheel the sandy-dirt path
under the palms, the path
that circles the island. They stop
to watch the waves, the white manes
like snowcap peaks of bluish green
mountains, break against coral.
The couple uncork
champagne, toast the seagulls
that circle like a necklace
of pearls, yet whose cries
sound like, "Thief, thief, thief."
The couple are from Iowa, out in the Pacific
for U.S. missile tests, for U.S.
Defense, for U.S. money—
the ocean is a new thing,
and they drink to it, drink to the salt
smell in the wind, and the
crabs running sideways on sand.
Night comes with stars
like the lights of fishing boats
sailing through the universe
dropping nets to catch human desire.
The couple hug, and the man,
seduced slightly by alcohol
makes a joke about coconut trees.

A Marshallese boy watches them
as he walks home.

ROI-NAMUR

—conversation at the Outrigger Bar

You think this is bad?
Gets worse, much worse
wait till you're here a year with nothing
you might as well be on the moon
fishing in the dirt.
Yeah, we got these big satellites
biggest in the world they say
to spy on the Chinese, so what
I got to live on an island a mile long
less than a mile wide where the food
tastes like dead cat and the cook has a degree
in waste management. I'm from Brooklyn.
Out here you can't even eat Marshallese,
toxins in the reef fish will kill you.
Don't have a tolerance against it.
I'm not an alcoholic, you know,
just drink to pass the time
because you got to do something
and everyone has vices out here
some guys dive, some run, some
watch television all day
though AFN is U.S. propaganda
George W. shouting, "War on Terror"
"War on Terror" all day all night, in your dreams
until you are ready to puke.
Me, I drink. I'm from Brooklyn.
I say get an edge, drink and be
one with the moon, or the coconut trees
or the crashing waves or whatever.
Some Americans—they get girlfriends,
Marshallese girls.
You know girls from third island, Enniburr
they got no electricity, no running
water over there, and so these guys

will go get girls and bring them here
these Americans—some—got wives back in the
States. They're out here for a fling.
No big deal—right?
You know I saw this one guy painting
a young girl on the beach
in his shack, painting, and whistling
like he was Robinson Crusoe
and Friday was this young girl.
I'm told they ain't got a school on Enniburr,
or a teacher or volunteer tutor
you know I'm from Brooklyn, got a degree
in engineering. I could tutor math, you know
but hell, this language barrier.
I can't speak Marshallese.
I mean you have foreigners show up on your doorstep
nuke your islands and then they don't leave.
You got to talk with them somehow.
War on terror, war on terror.
We are the terror.
But hell, let me buy you another drink.
I've talked too much tonight.
The stars out here glitter like
specks of glass in sand, you might start to count
them just to pass the time. This is my second
year on the island. I'm not an alcoholic you know
I just drink for something to do.
Like General Grant between battles, I drink.

AT A SAUKOU BAR, POHNPEI

Darkness,
the night like a sealed coffin
except one candle:
a waitress brings drink—grey, murky:

"Saukou!"

Made of meshed roots:
a small tree—beaten
into pulp, mixed with rainwater.

I sip what looks like mud: grey, cloudy.
Taste of mint.

Two boys in the back, shirtless
dark skin
like logs gleam in moonlight tide.

They take turns with rocks
phallic stone in hands,
strike roots
against stone floor: clank-clank

clank-clank. One-two, one-two.
Splitting fibers, mashing roots.
Every five minutes:
they rest; they wash the roots, twist the roots

into mason jars. I drink.

"Americans don't like the effect," the local
pastor told me. "Saukou opens the mind.
Americans prefer alcohol's blare."

The dark. A waitress
brings a second, a third.

Sandals clap against floor.

Stone love:
clank-clank. The boys take turns.
Clank-Clank.

A vision comes:
one boy in back is someone I know
he strips an iguana, hangs the

meat to dry. My sister, the one I've never
met, bathes in the ocean. This is not a bar—
the night recognizes me

welcomes with sparks of stone.
The full moon, its heart—beats out sweat
on my body
the darkness of skin touches me.

What is this quiet shout, this celebration?
oh, my sister hug me, hug me
let the tree frogs sing different marches

Laughter in the foam of ocean waves
even fish make jokes.
This is an island, but only because
the mind perceives it, water

protects it. Clank-clank.

I ask for another cup.

RAINING FISH

Because I was an alcoholic
and shouldn't be drinking
I had to ask the girl for a beer.
She was nine. There existed a bad stare:
thunderstorm's black eye
covering the pink of dawn.
A fish jumped in the sky.
My words were extinct currency.
It was as if I was no longer adult.
No longer I, but reverted backwards
a child with edges of gray
coming into his brown hair.
Spring and fall colliding
trees with white blossoms and brown leaves.
I had to look to others to make
important decisions. I had to ask
to do things. I wasn't trusted
with my thoughts alone.
The girl wore lilacs over her ears.
She slapped my hand, "Enough,
for two hundred lifetimes," she said,
pointed towards a line of naked men
all flabby and near old, with round
stomachs, thin legs. Above them a sign:
"The dead becoming sober ghosts."
The alarm woke me: 6 a.m.
In my journal I wrote:
"I shall be a zombie in heaven
as I was on earth."
Out the window it rained fish.

AN OVERHEARD CONVERSATION OUTSIDE DENNY'S IN ANCHORAGE, 5 A.M.

Two Men Talking

You make a mistake,
you gotta eat it.
Have a mistake sandwich,
pour ketchup on it,
down it with a beer,
and go out, get on.
God knows I've made
enough mistakes
to lose a small war.
In fact, a former boss once said,
my anger was like a herd
of cattle in a stampede.
It produces a lot of damage
but nothing constructive,
and he fired me.
I've lost five jobs in five years,
been arrested twice for DUI.
I had sex with a 15-year-old,
who she swore she was 21.
Almost went to jail, twice.
I punched out my ex-wife,
and broke her boyfriend's nose,
smashed the windshield of their car
with my Pete Rose Louisville Slugger.
Now they're suing me.
I put a hole in my neighbor's
dog with a .22.
Lied to the cops until they found the shells.
Did thirty days and one hundred hours.
Mistakes, all mistakes,
and I still go out,
meet the world every day.
So you just remember,

whatever you've done
can't be that bad,
and ain't nothing,
ain't nothing is unforgivable.

THE VIOLENT EXTINCTION OF STARS

The stars: bright butterflies
captured against black cloth.
Their wings glitter, blink,
as they flap to get away.

*

Once, in a fight in the wrong
section of town, someone
smacked me with a bottle.
Skull splintered glass
—a shower of crystals with wings—
someone butterflied my head.
Instead of asking, "How many fingers?"
Said, "Find the Big Dipper."
Out the window, cool air dried the blood.

*

The violent extinction of stars,
dwarfing themselves, glowing
more intense, expanding, exploding
before they swallow themselves into scars.

DRINKING ALONE

These were the first years of an old life.
Back when booze kissed my face after work
and Mickey Mantle was my hero.
I could go anywhere and everywhere
alcohol waited to greet me, to escort
me to bed. We had long conversations
which started in the morning, lasted past dusk.
Alcohol would ask about my mother,
hold me when I cried, "she left,
she didn't love my father. He was sick."
Alcohol promised never to leave.
I got moody when people came around.
They could fuck off—who needed them.
My relationship with alcohol was private.
I would close the shutters, lock the door,
pour a drink, settle into evening.

These were the first years of an old life.
My wife was a bitch, and the cat screamed
when I hit it with empty bottles.
Bars became places of dark freedom.
Entering, I walked out of the cage.
Alcohol would put on jazz
say, "listen to Chet Baker's gold horn."
And I could hear myself,
that man knew something important,
but it got all mixed up, lost.

Days, I watched baseball, morning to
evening. Watched the quick bat of Hank
Aaron as he pounded a single into left,
and the liquor flowed through me—
ran the bases, stealing second, third
as I fixed another drink, laugh,
before the pitch-out by Tom Seaver.

My wife left. One morning I noticed
her shoes and threw them at a mirror.
I hated her for leaving,
but was not lonely.
Alcohol was with me, it held me.

I enjoyed the same recurring memories. Alcohol
would ask about my father as we cuddled.
The conversation was always the same.

These were the first years of an old life.

FROM K.'S MEMOIRS

It was during these years that I broke into morgues and cut off the index fingers of the dead. I never liked people pointing at me. That second finger was too bossy, too aggressive, too much of a dictator making others do things and often resembling a gun. Most of the dead didn't need this finger in life and I figured none needed it in death. For a while these fingers piled up in my basement on a shelf with my tools: saws, pliers, screwdrivers. Then, one day, I decided on a plan. I mailed fingers to former girlfriends with notes, "Dear Deidre, I love you so much I've cut off my finger to prove my love" or "Dear Becky, This is one of the fingers I used to touch you with. I thought you might want it for sentiment, put it in a jar of vinegar, show it off" or "Dear Laura, This little piggy went to the market, bloody, bloody." I watched the news and newspaper for reports about fingers missing or fingers being stolen but none appeared. I must have taken hundreds of fingers, and no one noticed, no one cared. Maybe they were happy that the index, the finger that picked noses, looked at people wrong was gone, but I was hooked. I started to live for fingers, the removal of fingers. I started to amputate all the fingers on the bodies I found. I went to funeral homes like I was a member of the grieving family. My eyes held real tears. When the wake was over, I'd beg the funeral director, "Please, just a couple more minutes. He was my brother." Then with a sharp knife—whack whack whack— I'd put them in a Ziploc bag and walk. I began to have dreams about fingerless men roaming the streets after midnight looking for my home. They would stand outside my door with stubby palms held over mouths and whisper, "He's in there. What should we do?" I moved often, disconnected my phone, tried to get away from the dreams but I was addicted and needed more and more and I could not get help. I hung out at beauty salons and watched people receive manicures. My mouth drooled. Watching made me itch in places you're not supposed to scratch, and I followed those people home, left notes on their doors, "Your fingers are so beautiful. I would like to kiss them. Suck them. Hold them. Send them to presidents of foreign nations as ambassadors." I placed ads in national papers: "Will pay good money for fresh fingers" and "Male, age 27, looking for anyone 18-35 with long thin fingers. Race, sex, and looks not important." Then one morning I woke, and my pinky was gone. On the coffee table a ransom note with the voice of a coffin: "We have your little finger. Your baby. We will make it talk and then we will make it dance. And then we will call it bad names like snot nose or lost little brat. Return our fingers or you'll never see the little bitch again." I quickly moved out of the city, moved into a little cottage in a woods—I did not think they could follow me—and began to dig up the recently buried of the farmlands and remove their fingers. These I sent to my favorite movie stars: "Dear Johnny Depp, here's a finger in the state of decomposing. Notice the black skin and how it is a little bloated. Notice how the nail has gone untrimmed. You are my favorite actor." "Dear J-Lo, here is a dead finger. Look at how the bone sticks out at the end and how the vein looks like a tiny silkworm. Will you have my baby?" The actors never wrote back. Then one-day weeks later, I received a hand in the mail. It was a former girlfriend's hand. If I remembered correctly, we dated for fourteen days and she had gone insane began seeing ghosts and spent time in and out of hospitals. Her note said: "Dear K., I have missed you these long years. I never quit thinking about you or loving you. Your gift was so kind. For your finger, here is my hand." The hand sits in a jar on my nightstand. It is my most cherished possession. I call the ex-girlfriend two or three times a week. We are making plans, big plans.

III. RIVER CHURCH

RIVER

Sweat mixed with dirt
moistens the bristles of beard—
shadows of untrimmed fields—
his forehead battered by rain and wind
as he sits there and drinks
himself into the foggy night.
A fan whirls slowly, creates a breeze,
barely dissipates the July heat.
We're in a cheap rundown,
a motel with walls of chipped blue—
paint peeled to show lifetimes,
guests upon guests traveling
into the gray of other places.
Windows plastered shut
to keep out the crickets and bugs,
to keep in the stale smoke.
In a cracked mirror, my father
lights a cigarette, releases
the lung fog, takes a sip of brown
laughter: his bourbon, the sour flare
in his gray eyes.
He stole me this morning from mother,
put his hands over my mouth
as I hung the laundry, dragged me
to the green '75 Plymouth,
locked me in the trunk and drove
away the blue of Sunday.
I banged and banged against metal.
Screaming reminded me
of a scarecrow in a wilted corn field,
blackbirds pecking out its eyes.

There's a knock at the door.
A young woman, 18 maybe,
with hair like October trees,
black eyes filled with grackles,

birds that storm the cottonwoods
in the fall. Their great numbers
taking over the sky, turning it dark.
I lay on the bed and watch as he
pulls her dress over her head,
and she glows naked—unashamed:
small skulls for breasts.
She smiles and turns for him,
turns so he can see all of her.
"I want you to kiss her," my father
tells her, nods at me.
"No," I shake. "Please," I say.
"It's okay," she says,
brushes the hair out of my face,
kisses my lips. "I'm gentle," she says,
and kisses me again—it is almost
pleasant, the wet touch
like a caress, like a "hello",
and I want to be liked, want to disappear
into her dark mouth, but she groans,
and I stare into the eyes
a gunshot has startled
the grackles and their wings flap
hard and violent—the trees are full:
flapping black wings, feathers floating.
I see my father behind her
thrusting himself in.
"Come on whore," he says,
slaps her ass. "Make love
to my daughter."

RIVER CHURCH

At the edge of cow pasture
beyond barb wire
near a bend in river,
a boarded-up church
in a forest of white oak, sycamore,
cottonwood, filled by songs:
sparrow, thrush, cardinal,
horned owl. The doors
sealed with plywood, windows splintered,
then barred. I walk here on mornings grayed
when river fog shrouds the trees.
I peer through iron slits
to watch Jesus still on the cross,
still being crucified and still waiting
for the followers to take him down,
so he may forgive them.
I ask, "Why do you wait?
Why are you so patient?"
Behind his head, an empty wasp
nest rasps a papery reply—*don't worry*
like an old man dying, but
it is the breeze, the summer wind
through the hollow shell.
Jesus remains still, still patient.

The story: the preacher
died of malaria—caught sudden one June—
his followers fled, believed he'd
been cursed by a witch, a woman
called Goat Mistress. He'd gone
to her shack to convert her, saying the glory
of God would save. She had laughed,
"No man or son of man will ever save me."
The preacher took sick two days later.
Died amid the groan of river boats
at the height of morning fog.

Buttercups and wild irises
grow in the church cemetery,
wooden markers faded, names
weathered into silence, erased by rain.
The preacher buried somewhere else, lost.
No-one comes but me.
I bring roses for the dead, a sickle
to cut the grass and weeds.
At one time they called this place
River Church.

BETWEEN BREATHS

The flood of the womb
when time was water
and we had gills.
I have wished to return,
I have tried to return,
tried holding my breath
in the muddy river
until my lungs burned
like a flame of gasoline
in the kitchen of an old house.
I exploded upward gasping
as the crows in the trees
gawked and laughed,
spectators at some festival.
I imagined a village
at river's bottom
peopled by the dead:
friends and family
I have not met.

KAREN

I am Karen called whore,
called slut, called drunk.
My story starts on Friday
August 20ʰ, 1954
Jake's Bar, Kentucky.
Underage, I sat on a stool,
2 p.m.—already drunk.
I could get all the drinks
I ever desired,
for I knew how to flirt
until a man's cock stiffened,
until he opened his wallet
bought me anything.
And yeah, I jacked-off some
in the backroom for cash.
What do I care—
it's an act,
physical manipulation,
and men were nice
when I did it.
On that day, fire lived
in the whiskey, and I drank it
as if drinking the sun
for I drank away the light.
Men came and hugged me,
fondled me, and I danced
with everyone, kissed everyone,
even an eighty-year-old man
with no teeth.
I told people
they could fuck me,
for what did I care.
My body was a church.
men could pray inside,
stick their truths inside

and find God.
Then thunder came,
took the lights.
The bartender kicked us out.
I walked home alone
and in the rain, I saw her:
The Goat Woman.
She stood by a scarecrow.
She removed her hood
to show me the horns.
The horns glowed in the rain.
Then as I slept
the house caught fire.
I dreamt that the sun
awoke in my house, blazed
the wood into flame and smoke,
and then she burst through the door,
carried me out through the flames
as I choked on black smoke.

KENTUCKY

The buzz-saw of cicadas
in the trees announces the heat
to the tobacco fields' dark green,
leaves the color
of some South Pacific sea.
You expect ships
to be buried underneath
with lost treasure:
Spanish doubloons, Roman coin.
Men have drowned in tobacco
in this town searching for it.
Cut the plants in the rain
and caught the sickness—
were sucked under by the shovels'
undertow and the preacher's feverish words.
They disappeared in thunder.
Tobacco fields hold many bones,
more than most graveyards,
for the living must grow
upon the dead.

THE PHOTOGRAPH

He ties me up.
Rips the blouse
to expose my breasts.
Clicks the camera—
the evil eye.
"Innocence and bondage," he says.
"Torture and violence,
breasts and tears.
This is what the world
secretly desires.
These are what men
think about in their closets."

NIGHT

My mother's open grave:
a ripped-open casket empty
coal colored dirt
earthworms wiggling
sky a black scar
like scorched earth after a fire blazed
across fields and woods
my father above the hole
looking down, shaking his head
as rain begins.

THE GOAT WOMAN'S DREAM

Led to a stake, tied by monks in black
my eyes, black, speak of forests
of snake poisons, falcon shouts
of wolfsbane bound under moon's dark,
of blind trout in cavern streams, pond frogs.
They pile log upon log, blocks great and small
reach my mid-thigh, to burn, to roast
to condemn for being woman and leading men.
"Repent" they say. "Confess your Devil relations."

Red pine split by slaves with shriek of axe
larch-heart that chars to a chalk-white glow.
Chips of white oak deluged from ash buckets.
They spit in my face, curse me, dance.
As torch touches crackling twig,
as dry grass curls with leap of flame,
fire releases hisses from wood pith:
wild moans of trunks once trees,
once free in caressing wind.
The crowd claps, crudely laughs
amazed how quickly I burn.
Pluck of guitar string, fragile hum of fiddle—
the world again rid of eminent evil.
Yet they see my lips blacken—bubble—proclaim:
"I will come back through the trees,
I will come back with horns, playing music.
Mother, forgive them, they know not what they do."

RIVER CHURCH CEMETERY

Sixteen wooden marks
with a hawthorn tree at center:
River Church Cemetery.
I care for the graves
because they are forgotten.
The nameless are easy to love.
They want nothing
except the past.
Yesterday I replaced the markers
with new treated lumber
sixteen pieces that I stole
from Old Henry—
as he slept his noon break—
I painted the marks white
white for the puffed clouds
that float jolly over the blue,
puffed out of God's tobacco pipe
as he relaxes, daydreams
herds of cows.
                    My father says
the nameless have no hands, no
voice, but I've heard them,
crickets in old drawers:
"We are here," they call.
I have made up their names
a rebirth of sorts—
Sarah, Jordan, Pete.
I ask them to forgive me, but it
makes it easier. I can say
I need to pull the weeds around
Tiffany's head, or I need to
replace Tom's roses. I care for these
wooden marks—because I can,
because I'm allowed,
because I have little to care for,
and the dead tell me their stories:

When the Union soldiers came
Mother hid me in the well.
The old black butler brought
me dinner. They shot
my father for having once
whipped a slave girl.

Stories, I ask to hear.

NOTHING BUT THE THUNDER

They left her at the altar
(*for that's where women belong*).
They left her crying under the cross.
They left her with a note:
You are too ugly, too barren, too stupid, too worthless.
They stole her money for she had been rich.
They stole her virginity for she had been pure.
Though purity has nothing to do with the flesh—
they did not tell her this.
They said she was like every woman: *hollow*.
They left her in an empty church
for her parents had been dead.
Left her alone with a priest
who was embarrassed.
Left her with nothing but the clouds.
And the woman
crawled into a closet to disappear.

WHISPERS FROM THE RIVER

The chatter of rain
as the river rises.
There are ghosts
in the waters.
They come—like fog—
looking for the living.

*

The scars on her chest:
roses fossilized
in rock—records of what
once existed. She hugs me
and it feels strange, for I notice
the absence, the soft flesh
replaced by hardness
disappeared into the rock
of graves, of namelessness.

Her breasts were like extra
faces that kissed me
when we hugged—her breasts
fed me and made me strong.
Her breasts held voices—
women's voices that spoke
beyond the river:
"We're in this together,
suck and be strong."

KAREN WITH GRACKLES IN HER EYES

Told me this in a dream:
when one owns a darling face
and breasts that appear to be
small birds trying to fly from the chest—
then one contains
ample ability to make friends.
Beware of men who want to nourish you.

THE GREY OF THE WORLD

My mother died on a rainy Thursday
in Paris, Kentucky. I heard
the whippoorwill and the mourning
dove at dawn, and when the sun
failed I knew time was a blue
heron flown North for summer.
I did not rise when the grackles
pecked me with their high twits
as if they knew something desperate:
tit tit tit tit tit. Then came the sounds of water:
rain, faces all watching.
Rain, hands all touching,
tapping like drums, the bones,
the skin—rain and rain and rain.
A thousand mouths all talking, all
saying: *This is the moment of nothing,*
the gray that is the world.
Rain like flies covering the body.
Rain of wet kisses that dissolve.
Rain, where we all disappear.
The gray where our names
are forgotten and we become faceless.
She died on a rainy Thursday
in Paris, Kentucky. I prayed
for flood, for the waters to rise,
sweep away the house.
I wanted to live in the womb again.

AFTER THE GOAT WOMAN LEFT

After the goat woman left me
I spent my days
in the back of a Greyhound—
going from city to city,
seeking solace in rundown
taverns in places like Milwaukee,
buying the cheapest on tap,
watching old men with shaking
hands drink pints of Wild
Irish Rose. Ants in their gardens
hollowing, hollowing out logs,
setting up the palace
for the queen. Oh, I knew
alcoholism, watched my father
suffer, liver bleeding
until whiskey plugged
his heart. His last days in
a hospital, doctors saying,
"Nothing we can do but ease the pain."
The pain. I remembered his wild days,
his screaming, "Goddamn kids,
messin' up my woman."
How he chased us around the house
with a two-by-four and we hid
under the bed till he passed out.

*

After his death,
my life became a quiet
piano solo—rain and words
like rain upon a wood roof.
Then I fell in love
with the goat woman—
her small horns
in my palms

as I kissed her
and her eyes opened:
the noise of a
truck stop—
semis shaking
the windows of a trailer.

We spent nights
drinking wine, listening
to Art Pepper's
Late Night Radio Show.

*

"Art Pepper yer on the air."
"Art?"
"Yes."
"My girlfriend's been abducted by aliens."
"Really?"
"Yes. They left 'em circles in my corn and all my
chickens died and I come home seeing lights in the sky,
right over my house and my girlfriend's gone without a
note. She always wanted to see an alien. Art, do they
have sex with our women up there?"
"Actually if your woman was abducted—she probably
was an alien to begin with…"
"You mean I've been having sex with an alien."
"Yes, if I were you I'd get tested for some sexually
transmitted disease."
"Sex disease?"
"Yes, some Alien virus that has no cure."
"Goddamn." Click.
"Art Pepper yer on the air."
"Art, I'm a vampire from Milwaukee."

Nights the goat woman disappeared like an abduction.
Disappeared like my alcoholic father
into a time where minutes fell like rain—
all at once.

RIVER CHURCH KENTUCKY

The old church holds rats.
They scamper across the floor,
sniffing the air—often they
look up at Jesus on the cross
as if he calls them,
proclaims them his followers.
Proclaims them his congregation.
The rats quickly move on,
ignore his voice, his stare,
ignore his commands.
Resume the search for food.

BECKY SPEAKS OF THE GOAT WOMAN

A man licked my horns
as I bit his nipple—wine,
rich and red,
flowered into my mouth.
Under a butternut tree,
three men played poker,
drank whiskey.
Their breaths, filled with fire,
cursed women
for they saw only flesh.
Tongues clashing against
teeth, waves against rock,
saying, "Bitches, all of them, bitches.
They all need to be fucked."
Suddenly, a roar
filled the forest.
A naked woman,
with the head of a goat,
with the speed of a horse,
appeared out of the pines.
She butted the men to death.
Impaled their guts on her horns.
Spread the intestines
for the crows.